Secret Tu

Activity B

Calling all Moshling hunters! Greetings, Buster Bumblechops, super Moshling expert, here. Now, although I am fangtastic at catching these tricky little critters, I might just need your help today, because a few of them are proving more than a bit difficult to catch. Keep your eyes peeled (not literally!) in the pages of this book for Zack Binspin, Bobbi SingSong and O'Really, they're teeny-weeny masters of hide-and-seek. Happy hunting!

OME TO

RO CITY

Can you remember where you put the Monster item?

Fried Egg Rug

Deep under Monstro City's streets lie the creepy, damp and dark Underground Tunnels, where strange creatures live in green slime-filled streams. The Underground Tunnels are also home to the coolest venue in town – the Underground Disco – where you can strut your hairy stuff, mingle with the stars and be insulted by the City's meanest judge and one and only talent scout, Simon Growl!

The Underground Tunnels Quiz

1
What's the name of the tiny monster behind bars who is always crying?

2
How many bats hang around the Underground Tunnels? And what are their names?

3
Name the two little creatures that live in the green murky waters of the Underground slime streams.

4
How many purple mushrooms grow outside the scary door by Ecto's Cave?

5
How many pots of paint are there by Art Lee's graffiti wall?

Take this tricky test to see if you know your
green slime from your latest monstrous disco diva!

UNDERGROUND DISCO

10
What's written
on Bubba's arm
under his heart
tattoo?

9
Who are the three
Moshlings in the front
row of paparazzi,
taking photos?

8
What lies on the
stone floor in front
of the Underground
Disco entrance?

6
Who is the
tattooed bouncer that
guards the entrance
to the Underground
Disco?

7
What is the symbol
on the stone cave
entrance that Bonkers
sits in front of?

Who is hiding behind the scary monster door and what are they up to? Crack this slimey code to find out.

The Underground Tunnels may be one of the coolest (and dampest!) places to hang out, but they also provide the ideal dark hiding places for the dastardly Dr. Strangeglove and his evil minions, the Glumps!

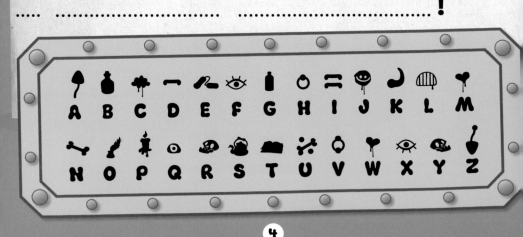

He's mean, he's grumpy, who knows where he shops for his trousers, and he never has a good word to say about anyone, but when it comes to spotting talent Simon Growl is the top monster! Hang out with the Growl Crowd and some of that Growl Factor might just rub off on you!

The 'Growl' Factor

Add up the scores to see who Simon Growl's next monSTAR act will be!

12 **4** **6**   **15** **9** **15**   **10** **7** **3**

A. **B.** **C.**

3 **5** **2**   **8** **8** **3**

D. **E.** **?**

Monster looks can be deceiving. Take Bubba the bouncer. He is a BIG bruiser, but under that decorated body is a nimble disco dancer and talented artist. If he ever gets a day off, ask him to show you his moves and his roarsome body art.

Bubba's Terrific Tattoo Art

Dig deep into that monstermental brain of yours and use the space here to design a new hair-raising tattoo for the big guy. Go Moshi mad!

Art Lee's graffiti art may only be an underground movement at the moment, but he is producing monster works of pop art all over those slimey tunnels and caves! He hopes that some Moshi will discover him and put his art above ground in the Googenheim Gallery. Could he be the next Danksy?

Art Lee's Pop Art

Get inspired by this mushroom monster artist's latest scrawls on the tunnel walls, and draw your own pop art piece here.

Oh, Ecto! You've been wobble-plasmu'd!

Woo-oo-oo! Who you gonna call? Spookybusters? No, put down that mobile, this is one friendly Fancy Banshee. Ecto sure is cute, but hugs are out or you'll be in lots of wobbly trouble.

Ask these hairy guys - they all touched that shimmering cape of electrified wobble plasma and got well and truly Ecto'd! Turn them back the right way to see who they are.

1.

2.

3.

4.

5.

6.

Batty Spot the Difference

The Underground Tunnels' battiest residents, Wing, Fang, Screech and Sonar, were exiled from Ecto's Cave after terrifying Monstro City residents. They now spend their nights flapping through the tunnels listening out for gossip to report to *The Daily Growl*.

Take a good goggle at these two pictures. Can you spot ten differences between them? See if you can also spot something gossip-worthy. The flappy foursome arc already on the case!

9

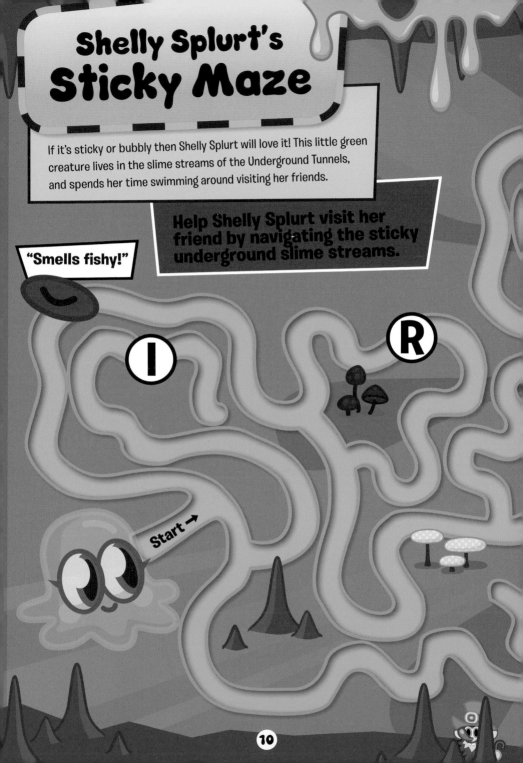

Shelly Splurt's
Sticky Maze

If it's sticky or bubbly then Shelly Splurt will love it! This little green creature lives in the slime streams of the Underground Tunnels, and spends her time swimming around visiting her friends.

Help Shelly Splurt visit her friend by navigating the sticky underground slime streams.

"Smells fishy!"

Start →

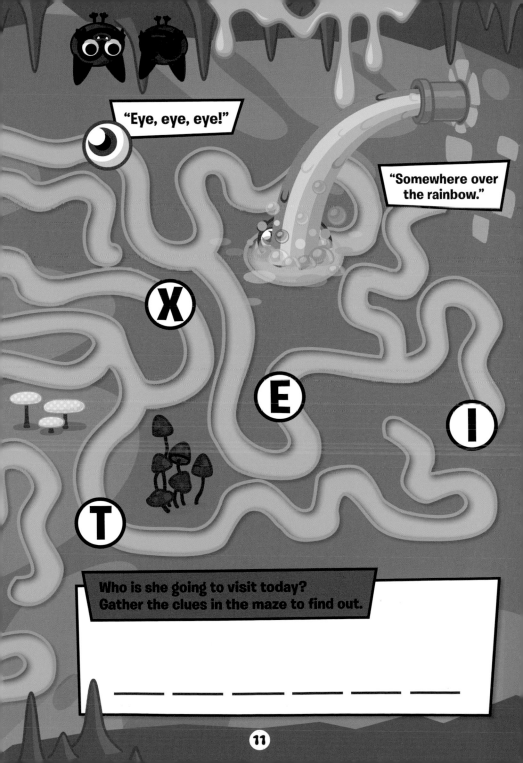

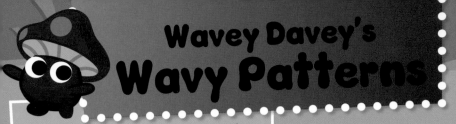

Wavey Davey's
Wavy Patterns

Give a high-five to this happy little chappy. Wavey by name and wavey by nature, Wavey Davey's favourite pastime is, yes, you've got it, WAVING! He lives down in the Tunnels with his friend Snooze Cruise, who is hardly ever awake to wave back.

Draw the picture in the box that completes the patterns below.

Simon Growl's
Hui. y C.ROSSwo. u

Let's face it, this grumpy pop genius always has a CROSS word to say. And his hair isn't any better! Fill in this not-cross-at-all CROSSword puzzle, to remind the Growlster how lucky he is to be part of the coolest (and we are talking D A M P!) and darkest (that's FUNKY to those in the know) Underground scene.

Across:

1. What is the Sandy Drain, where Simon and his showbiz pals hang out? (5)
4. This gloved C.L.O.N.C. member has a musical side (2, 12)
5. The bouncer who stands guard outside the Underground Disco (5)
7. Jollywood's biggest star!

Down:

2. _ _ _ _ Fangs is Simon's fellow judge (4)
3. The MopTop Tweenybop whose hair is too long! (4, 7)
6. Moshimo City's dancing megastar! (5,3)
8. This Flashy Fox loves to rap (6)

Where are the Techies?

Fill in the number of times you can find each Moshling in the circles below.

Simon Growl's
Bad Hair Day!

As all monsters know, some days when you get out of bed and look in the mirror, you get a hair-raising fright! Yes, you are having a MONstrous bad hair day! Even that growly pop-meister Simon Growl needs a little help with his huffy hair. Give the Growlster's hair a face-over by drawing six different funny faces here. You never know, you might be the first to put a smile on Mr. Growl's face!

Answers

Page 1
Zack Binspin is hidden on page 5; Bobbi SingSong is on page 8; O'Really is on page 10 and the Fried Egg Rug is on page 12.

Pages 2-3
The Underground Tunnels Quiz
1. Cry Baby.
2. Four. Wing, Fang, Screech and Sonar.
3. Trixie Fish and Shelly Splurt.
4. Ten.
5. Three. Pink, green and white paint.
6. Bubba - he is a prominent tattoo artist as well as a night club bouncer.
7. An eye.
8. A large red Growly Bear Rug.
9. Flumpy, Peppy and Pooky.
10. Mom.

Page 4
Underground Codebreaker
The secret message is:
Dr. Strangeglove has sent Squiff down to the tunnels to let rip with a Squiffy Stinkbomb!

Page 5
The 'Growl' Factor
Dr. Strangeglove has the 'G' Factor with a monstrous score of 39.

Page 8
Oh, Ecto! You've been wobble-plasma'd!
1. CocoLoco, 2. Mustachio, 3. Jessie, 4. Ruby Scribblez, 5. Snozzle Wobbleson, 6. Sweet Tooth.

Page 9
Batty Spot the Difference

Pages 10-11
Shelly Splurt's Sticky Maze

Shelly is going to visit Trixie.

Page 12
Wavey Davey's Wavy Patterns

Page 13
Simon Growl's Hairy CROSSword

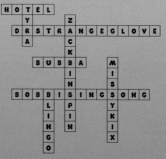

Page 14
Where are the Techies?

3 Gabbys
1 Holga
2 Nippers
2 Wurleys